BRITISH RAIL
TRACTION
MAINTENANCE DEPOTS
1974–1993

Part 1: Northern England

MICHAEL RHODES

Published by Platform 5 Publishing Ltd,
52 Broadfield Road, Sheffield, S8 0XJ. England.

Printed in England by The Amadeus Press, Cleckheaton, West Yorkshire.

ISBN: 978 1 909431 68 3

Above: On 19 April 1987 Sunderland shed was full for the weekend. From left to right at the front of the old steam shed were 56119, 56128 and 56112. Behind them in the stygian gloom were 56129, 56131, 56123 and 56122, along with 08442 at rest outside.

Front cover: On 1 August 1990, Class 47s active and withdrawn are seen at the east end of the impressive Tinsley depot building. In the foreground is 47293 in Railfreight Distribution livery with 47120 resting against its buffers. Behind these are 47009, 47012, 47338 and 47445, some of which are out of sight.

Back cover: On a visibly cold 27 February 1986, 31468, 47093 and 56120 stand outside the two-track refuelling shed at Gateshead. The author had perched himself in this location to photograph the afternoon trip freight that travelled from Tyneside Central freight depot to Tees Yard which on that occasion was hauled by 47302.

Previous page: On 23 September 1980, 31228, 45036 and 20210 stand at the east end of Tinsley depot. The litter between the tracks was typical of the time as were the diesel spillages between the stabling tracks.

CONTENTS

INTRODUCTION

Many of us remember the halcyon days of trainspotting in the 1970s and 1980s. Steam may have gone, but there was still the excitement that the large variety of motive power brought and the "Locoshed Directory" published by Ian Allan to encourage us to seek out the locomotives that could be found on shed. We called it "shed bashing" back in 1970s. We never had a permit and we always sought the best advice as how to "bunk" the shed and collect all the numbers. It seems madness in today's health & safety, woke and politically correct world but it was a wonderful time.

As a school boy living in South Wales, for me Saturdays were all about trainspotting. Would we go to Cardiff for the morning, or if we had saved enough money from our paper round to have a day out, we would get up early and head somewhere more exotic. By exotic, I mean anywhere outside South Wales! Favourite trips were a day to London to visit the sheds at Stratford and Finsbury Park, and then maybe Old Oak Common or Hither Green before a late train home. The commonest trip we made was north to Derby for Toton depot and this was sometimes combined with a trip to Tinsley in Sheffield, or to Bescot and Saltley in the Midlands. On three occasions, these trips coincided with Derby Works open day and another long but enjoyable day out was to Crewe Works Open Day, which was a high point in the calendar.

More locally there was an interesting promotion in South Wales during the 1970s which allowed a half-price return ticket after 16.00 on Saturday, enabling a trip to Bristol to be made for just a few pence! We cheated and left Cardiff half an hour early, arriving in Newport to catch the Newport to Gloucester train which stopped at Severn Tunnel Junction. My recollection is that this left a few minutes after the 16.00 deadline. Having arrived at "STJ" we did the shed there and then hopped on the next Cardiff to Bristol train to do Bath Road. Having started the trip with a 15.00 visit to Canton, we managed three major sheds on a Saturday afternoon! The first of these trips to Bristol ended in disaster when a British Transport Policeman (BTP) spotted us sneaking off the end of Platform 10 at Bristol and came after us into Bath Road depot. I didn't realise that my two fellow spotters had been to Bristol before and knew the way out from the back of the depot, near the old turntable. I did not though, and was arrested on my return to Platform 10. A few days later I was visited at home by the BTP, after having warned my parents about my arrest and I received a stern telling off. Interestingly, whilst my parents were quite strict, all this visitation did to my father was encourage him to regale me with stories from his youth when he had been caught for poaching fish in a reservoir near his home in Lancashire. Much to my relief, this unfortunate episode didn't lead to an end to my outings, just more care on my part not to get caught!

During the early 1970s, spending time on Cardiff General station (as it was known until 1973), one quickly picked up information from older spotters about which sheds were easy to get round and which were difficult. In general, the view seemed to be that the Scottish Region was the most friendly to railway enthusiasts, whilst the North Eastern Region was the harshest. Certainly Holbeck, Healey Mills and Gateshead were notoriously difficult to bunk without getting caught. Another depot which was always a challenge was Finsbury Park. In contrast, my "home" depot of Cardiff Canton often had dozens of spotters unofficially looking round at the weekend, as some of the images in this book demonstrate. In April 1973, having more or less exhausted the options for day trips from Cardiff, I asked if I might stay with my grandparents for a week in Lancashire and my wish was granted. Myself and a friend called "Piff" (both still aged 12) headed off by train to Manchester and then by bus to Great Harwood. We were looked after right royally by my grandparents, treated to ham, egg and chips every evening and given sandwiches every day for lunch. Not only did this allow us to visit all the depots in the North West, but it enabled our first visit to Scotland. I have written about this adventure before; we went to Preston, leaving Rishton early and whilst my parents and grandparents thought we were spending the day in Preston, we bought half (child) day returns to Edinburgh on the newly introduced electric service north from Preston. My grandparents did wonder why we were so late home, but we just said we'd had an excellent day. It was not until a couple of decades later that the truth about the day out to Edinburgh came out over a Sunday lunch with my parents! Not only did we have family in Lancashire, but we had different friends from our church who had moved to Sheffield, Middlesborough and Edinburgh, all of whom were happy to have a teenage trainspotter stay for a few days during the school

holidays. Consequently, most depots in the UK were visited several times during my school days.

In addition to depots where both repairs and refuelling took place, there were many stabling points dotted about the country. Some of these had more locomotives on site than the major depots did. Two that immediately spring to mind are Guide Bridge and Warrington Arpley, both of which were packed at weekends. Stabling points were also the key to tracking down elusive shunting locomotives and the 1973 publication "Shunter Duties" by the Inter City Railway Society was an invaluable aid for doing this. The aim of every trainspotter in the 1970s was to "clear" British Rail (BR), meaning to see every locomotive, or indeed every locomotive, diesel multiple unit (DMU) and electric multiple unit (EMU). I managed to clear BR in 1978 when I finally saw 25321 on Carlisle's Kingmoor depot! Of course clearing BR was a moving target, as new stock was introduced and older locomotives were withdrawn. By the summer of 1978 however, my interest was increasingly focussed on photography and much less on number collection, so much so that from 1980 I recorded what I photographed in my notebooks but no longer recorded every locomotive I saw. After this change in emphasis, a few of my pictures were published in 1978, first in Modern Railways and then in the Locoshed book itself. The trainspotter in me was still there, as I managed to photograph just about every Class 37 and thanks to the late Bob Ranson, I completed my collection with his 1965 image of D6983, which was the first Class 37 to be written off after it was badly damaged in a collision that year.

Having stopped taking numbers by 1980, I still found that I visited sheds, but mainly to take pictures. I realised over the decades that I had accidentally photographed just about all the Class 56s, 58s and 60s and even today I keep a record to see if I have accidentally photographed all the Class 66s!

The reader might well ask why the period from 1974 to 1993 has been chosen. Its start was dictated by the time of my early depot visits and its end was determined by several factors. Concerns about trespassing were becoming greater as we entered the 1990s. At the same time I was no longer a student or junior doctor, but was working as a lecturer in Surgery in Cardiff from 1992 and from then I started to become concerned that getting arrested for visiting an engine shed would be irresponsible. Palisade fencing was also appearing around depots and I can remember finding entry into Canton and Immingham suddenly being impossible due to the new fencing. The tradition of "shed bashing" was accepted as normal in the 1960s, tolerated in the 1970s and had turned into trespass with consequences by the early 1990s.

This is the first volume in a three-part series of my photographs of British depots. It covers Northern England and further volumes covering Southern & Central England and finally Wales & Scotland will follow. The series is not a text book or historical summary of all the depots, but rather a recollection of hundreds of hours of a misspent youth. Some major depots hardly feature because I made few visits to them or didn't take any photographs while there. On the other hand, my "home" depots, such as Gateshead, March Whitemoor and Cardiff Canton are perhaps over represented because I lived near each of these at different times. Hopefully this selection of images will bring back many happy memories for those of us who enjoyed the freedoms of trainspotting in the 1970s and 80s.

Michael Rhodes
Thurston, 2022

THE NORTH WEST

CARLISLE KINGMOOR

Beginning with England's most north-westerly depot, Kingmoor was a 55-minute walk from Carlisle's Citadel station, but there was the option of taking a bus as I recall. The last stretch of the journey to Kingmoor was along the marvellously named Etterby Scaur. Even further north and a 90-minute walk from the station was Carlisle New Yard stabling point. This opened in 1962 when the new Kingmoor Yard was commissioned and it serviced the many freight locomotives that passed through the massive Kingmoor hump yards. The main Kingmoor depot did not open until 1968, when the steam depot on the opposite side of the West Coast Main Line (WCML) closed. Kingmoor was phased out of use in 1987 when it lost its allocation of locomotives but was subsequently taken on by Direct Rail Services (DRS) in 1998. The company refurbished it and still uses the site today. As for the New Yard stabling point, this closed in 1984, three years after the remaining hump at Kingmoor was taken out of use. The building survived for nearly a decade without any railway tracks but has long since been demolished. A second major stabling point linked to Kingmoor depot was Workington, where in the 1970s locomotives were stabled in the old steam shed. By 1981, these were mainly stabled in a bay platform within the station. Citadel station was also used to stable locomotives and this became more commonplace once the New Yard fuelling point had closed.

Class	Locos
08	08106, 08132, 08352, 08419 & 08912
24 & 25	24002, 25041, 25053, 25091, 25147, 25151, 25190, 25191, 25192, 25201, 25317 & 25322
37	37165 & 37193
40	40076, 40097, 40106, 40120, 40131, 40136, 40159, 40162 &40186
45	45002 & 45013
47	47083, 47357, 47363 & 47442
50	50031, 50034 & 50036
81–87	85009, 86015, 86042, 86214, 86229, 87003, 87005, 87017, 87021, 87023, 87025 & 87033

Table 1: Locos present at Carlisle Kingmoor and New Yard on 19 August 1974.

Below: On 18 July 1984, from left to right 08569, 25202 and 25044 line up in the late evening sun at the north end of Kingmoor depot.

Above & below: Two aspects of the new Kingmoor depot are illustrated in these views. Provision was made to refuel and clean a small diesel multiple unit (DMU) fleet at the depot. On 10 July 1978, three of the two-car Class 108 units used on the Cumbrian Coast route sit beside TDB975227, a departmental single-car DMU. The other units are numbered 50964 & 56247, 50956 & 56238 and 56234 & 50959. The second image taken from the east side of the WCML on derelict ground formerly occupied by Kingmoor steam depot shows 84003 and 40127 at the north of the main shed. The overhead wires extended to the entrance of the building which was constructed with clearances that could allow conversion to an electric depot at a future date.

Above: On 10 July 1978, 40159 lines up with 45042, 47255 and 47147 to the east of the single track fuelling shed at Kingmoor New Yard.

Above: This overall view of the Kingmoor Yard stabling point was taken on 18 July 1984. The Up Hump Tower is visible in the distance above the single track shed and the 48 Up Sorting Sidings are spread across the horizon. It was possible to identify 27066 outside the fuelling shed and to its right 25196, behind which was 26026. Also present were a couple of electric locomotives, a pair of 25s and a 37.

Left: The 12-road steam depot just south of the station at Workington lost its steam allocation in 1968. It was never modernised for diesel use, but as this image shows it continued to be used to stable diesels and refuel them until at least 1983. On 5 July 1983 an unidentified Class 40 stands on the only road left with a servicing pit, whilst the rest of the depot was full of Covhop wagons that were stored and not being repaired.

Above: On 23 June 1981, most of the locomotives were stabled at Workington station, rather than in the old steam depot. In the bay platform that points south, from left to right are 47229, 47429, 40015 and 25135.

BARROW-IN-FURNESS

Above: There was a major locomotive depot at Barrow-in-Furness which survived long enough to be given a TOPS code, BW. The shed closed in 1977 when refuelling and servicing of diesel locomotives was transferred to the carriage sidings north of the station. Following the collapse of heavy industry around Barrow-in-Furness during the 1970s and 80s, few locomotives are now used in the area. During the 1980s, the few freight workings that remained utilised the locomotives stabled at Barrow station, such as those seen here on 26 June 1981, when 25168 and 25089 were on the stabling point.

WIGAN SPRINGS BRANCH AND WARRINGTON ARPLEY

When Wigan Springs Branch diesel depot opened in 1968, it was the largest diesel depot in the Liverpool Division. It was a 35-minute walk from Wigan North Western station. My recollection from several visits between 1974 and 1992 is that staff were friendly and security was relatively lax, as the images of the depot suggest. Springs Branch provided motive power for the freight traffic that ran between Liverpool, Wigan, Warrington and Blackburn. By the 1990s, only a vestigial wagonload service from Warrington Arpley Yard and the coal traffic between local collieries and Fiddlers Ferry Power Station remained. As a result, the original diesel depot was threatened with closure in 1992, but survived as a northern base for Transrail until 1997. After this, day to day servicing of freight locomotives was undertaken at a new two track depot that opened at the north end of Warrington Arpley Sorting Sidings. English, Welsh & Scottish Railway (EWS) then used Springs Branch to stable locomotives well into the 21st century and scrapped several 47s and 56s there. The Springs Branch site was later repurposed as a maintenance facility for Northern's multiple units in 2019.

Warrington Arpley was the primary stabling point for locomotives from Wigan Springs Branch depot. It was a five-minute walk from Warrington Bank Quay station and most locomotives could be spotted from the adjacent road. Once the new shed in Arpley Yard opened in 1997, the old stabling point closed and the area has now become derelict ground. There was easy access from a lane at the eastern end of the old stabling point, where a closer inspection of the locomotives stabled was possible. Other outposts of Wigan Springs Branch were at Preston, Blackburn, Blackpool and Horwich Works.

Class	Locos
08	08303, 08328, 08340 & 08846
25	25109, 25112, 25140, 25269, 25279, 25320 & 25317
40	40015, 40055, 40082, 40090, 40136, 40144, 40175, 40177, 40178 & 40179
47	47287
50	50040

Table 2: Locos present at Wigan Springs Branch on 17 August 1975.

Class	Locos
08	08126, 08337, 08423 & 08624
24	24057
25	25110, 25290, 25291 & 25307
40	40087, 40104 & 40175

Table 3: Locos present at Warrington Arpley on 11 June 1977.

Below: On 24 September 1982, 47316, 40131, 08342 and 25113 line up outside the maintenance shed at Wigan Springs Branch. Also present on the depot that day were 25079, 25206, 40022, 40033, 40034, 40058 and 40096.

Above: 40096 is being jacked up in the main shed at Wigan Springs Branch on 24 September 1982, whilst 25079 undergoes a minor A examination as it stands between several other locomotives.

Above: 40022, which carries the less than official nameplate "Laconia" beneath the bolt holes where the original nameplate was attached, undergoes maintenance within Wigan Springs Branch depot on 25 September 1982. Also recorded on the depot that day were 08342, 25079, 25113, 25206, 25240, 40034, 40058, 40096, 40131 and 47315.

Above: On
17 September 1984,
25069 and 25321 contrast
inside the maintenance
shed at Springs Branch.

Right & above right:
In 1992, the future of the
depot at Springs Branch
was in the balance. The
main maintenance shed
was filled predominantly
with wagons. The only
locomotives inside on
27 March 1992 were
60061 and 60072, both
of which were used on
the MGR trains that
transferred coal from
Bickershaw and Parkside
Collieries to Fiddlers
Ferry Power Station.
Outside meanwhile, on
the tracks formerly covered
by the main steam depot,
from left to right were
47350, 47368 which was
obscuring 08468 behind it
and 47191, 20081, 20016,
20057, 20154, 20073 on
the right.

Left: During the "Indian Summer" for Wigan Springs Branch, on 28 September 1984 56009 and 56031 stand alongside 31160 inside the maintenance shed.

Above: On 10 July 1992 the stabling point at Arpley contains an interesting variety of traction, which from left to right comprises of 20059, 20168, 47374, 60069, 31324, 20057 and 20154.

Left: In 1994 and 1995, Springs Branch was responsible for 85 locomotives, including 15 Class 08 shunters and 51 Class 31s. The line up on the sidings of the former steam depot on 29 August 1994 reflects this with several 31s present, including 31262, 31301 & 31512, along with a line of 08s, half a dozen withdrawn 20s (out of view) and 47193.

Class	Locos
08	08265, 08297 & 08624
25	25074, 25105, 25154 & 25163
40	40001, 40090 & 40091
47	47353

Table 4: Locos present at Warrington Arpley on 23 June 1979.

Top & above: In the first image 40001 is seen arriving at Arpley stabling point after having travelled from the marshalling yard on 23 June 1979. The second photo shows the locos that were stabled in the sidings on that particular Saturday and these are summarised in Table 4.

Above: This similar view of Arpley stabling point, taken a couple of years earlier on Friday 10 June 1977, shows it when the sidings were relatively empty. From left to right are 40009, 40104, 40149, 47266, 25110 and 25168.

Below: Just after midday on 25 September 1982, the small stabling point adjacent to Blackburn station contained 25276, 37152 and 08129 which is just visible behind 37152. The 37 had arrived from Healey Mills earlier that day with the daily mixed freight from the hump yard there and would return later with empty coal wagons for the Yorkshire Coalfield. To the right of the locos, the Class 104 DMU that will form the 12.33 to Manchester Victoria sits in the bay platform.

BIRKENHEAD MOLLINGTON STREET

The depot at Mollington Street was only a ten-minute walk from Birkenhead Central station. The steam shed was reroofed in 1961 and a modern diesel depot built a few years after that. The depot handled traffic in and around Birkenhead Docks and also from the petrochemical plants at Ellesmere Port and Stanlow. When the depot closed in 1985, locomotive stabling for local freight workings moved to Ellesmere Port Yard. Two sample observations at the depot from 1974 are shown in Table 5.

Class	Locos on 21 August 1974	Locos on 27 December 1974
08	08078 & 08490	08079
24	24045, 24052,	24059 & 24075
25	25214, 25260 & 25319	25114, 25119 & 25278
40	None	40001, 40082, 40182, 40186 & 40189
47	47517	47241, 47350 & 47353

Table 5: Locos present at Birkenhead Mollington Street on two dates in 1974.

Above: On 8 August 1975 40079 stands outside Birkenhead Mollington Street's modern diesel shed, while 08069 undergoes repairs inside the building. To its right, 25288 stands in front of the re-roofed steam shed. Also present on the shed that day was 24030.

Right: 56134 is stabled alongside 60048 and 60038 at Ellesmere Port on 22 December 1996. The signing on point and stabling sidings closed in 2000, but the crew building was still intact under the bushes as recently as 2021.

Above: On New Year's Day in 1980, 25154, 25036, 25301 and 25287 line up next to 47366 inside the old Great Western Railway's steam shed at Mollington Street. 40050, 40116, 40126, 47191 and 47318 were also found at the depot that day.

ALLERTON

The depot at Allerton was mainly responsible for the upkeep of DMUs and shunting locomotives. Opened in 1960, the new five-road shed could accommodate five four-car units. The depot was a ten-minute walk from Allerton station and relatively easy to visit. The downside of visits to Allerton was that most of its shunters would be scattered across other sites; the 08s would be stabled at Warrington, Glazebrook, Runcorn, Ditton, Northwich, Edge Hill, Liverpool Docks, Garston, Speke Yard and Liverpool Lime Street station. This meant that visits to the depot often yielded only a fraction of its allocation.

The major stabling points linked to Allerton, where both shunters and main line locomotives could be found, were Edge Hill, Speke Junction (which replaced Garston Docks in the late 1970s), Northwich and Lime Street station.

Class	Locos
02	D2852, 02001, 02003 & 02004
08	08300, 08431, 08688, 08887, 08917 & 08939
81	81014

Table 6: Locos present at Allerton on 8 August 1975.

Above & below: These two images show 02001, 02003 and 02004 at Allerton on 8 August 1975. The trio were the only three members of the 20-strong class to remain in service long enough to be given TOPS numbers and had only been formally withdrawn two months before these photographs were taken.

Above: As mentioned above, Allerton predominantly cared for DMUs. On 8 August 1975 three sets are seen lined up in the cleaning sidings, which is where units were parked between duties so that rubbish could be cleared, toilets serviced and the water tanks refilled.

Below: On 27 December 1974, Garston Docks was host to 08679, 08838, 08884, 08895 and 08924. Also present were 25287, 40093, 40127 and 40188, the latter two of which are illustrated here. Behind the photographer was an electrified siding in which 83006 and 87034 were held.

Above: By 1980, the sidings on the dockside at Garston were no longer used to stable locomotives and these were instead kept in a siding adjacent to Garston Junction signal box, at the west end of Speke Junction Yard. On New Year's Day 1980, 08291 is captured alongside 40182 and 40022, with 47266 sandwiched between them. Also present but out of view were 08289, 08628 and 08931.

Left top & left: The 1876 vintage steam depot at Northwich was used as a diesel stabling point from the mid-1960s. It closed as a train crew depot in 1984 and was finally demolished in 1991. The first image shows 40063 standing outside on the fuelling siding on 29 June 1983. Just over a year later, on 20 September 1984, which was just weeks before the depot effectively closed, 20185, 20153 and 47380 are stabled within the old steam shed. The ancient coach behind the 20s is a survivor from the pre-BR era that was being used as a tool store at the time.

Above: On 10 March 1984, 40012 & 40001 are found alongside 47330 at the buffer stops in Lime Street. The station's central storage lines were removed in recent years when it was remodelled.

MANCHESTER DEPOTS

The Locoshed Directory lumped all the depots in Manchester together. The three major depots were Longsight in the south, Newton Heath to the north and Reddish in the east which serviced the DC electric trains used on the Woodhead Route. Several stabling points were linked to the main depots and these included Guide Bridge and Buxton which was a significant location in its own right. Manchester's Piccadilly and Victoria stations were also minor stabling points.

LONGSIGHT

On the southern side of the city was the depot at Longsight which was a full hour's walk from Manchester Piccadilly, although one could catch a bus from the station approach to nearby Levenshulme. The depot serviced AC electric and diesel locomotives, as well as DMUs in a hotch potch of buildings. The diesel servicing shed was a six-road building constructed in 1957, originally for steam locomotives. The old LNWR 11-track carriage shed was electrified in 1960 and a small two-track electric locomotive depot was opened the same year.

Above: This image is from an atrocious negative and even after half an hour of work in Photoshop, it still has many blemishes. It shows the shed foreman shooing a young Rhodes off the premises on 11 August 1975. Clayton–built Class 17 8598 worked as a departmental locomotive between 1972 and 1978, having previously been at Gateshead and in Scotland where it worked local freight services. It was officially withdrawn in 1971 but then spent much of its latter years in and around Longsight depot.

Below: On 1 January 1975, 85002 and 85030 are seen at the north end of the 11-road carriage shed. The other locomotives on shed at Longsight that day are listed in Table 7.

Class	Locos
08	08205, 08611 & 08914
25	25086 & 25244
40	40012, 40030, 40043 & 40126
47	47364
81–87	E3023, 81018, 81021, 83002, 83003, 83005, 85002, 85030, 86205, 86233, 87020 & 87035

Table 7: Locos present at Longsight on 1 January 1975

Above: On 10 June 1977 40111 stands at the north end of Longsight's diesel servicing shed. Behind it is 47348 and 40030 is just visible on the right. In total, there were five electric locomotives, eight main line diesels and a solitary 08 on shed that day.

Above: A Class 104 DMU on a Buxton service passes on the main line, while 85033 and 84001 stand outside the two-track electric depot on 10 June 1977.

These three images show the diesel servicing area on 3 November 1983. Firstly, 40001 stands at the southern end of the shed, adjacent to the refuelling road. Inside 40080 is visible alongside a variety of DMUs that are being serviced. Finally, 40086, 40080 and 40057 are photographed together on the heavy maintenance tracks at Longsight.

NEWTON HEATH

The depot at Newton Heath was only a five-minute walk from Dean Lane station and even though the Locoshed Directory advised catching various buses to visit the depot, travelling by train was by far the easiest way to get there. The depot retained a steam allocation until early in 1968, yet between 1958 and 1968 it was gradually altered to cater first for DMUs and then for main line diesels. By the early 1970s, there was a long four-road shed for units, a three-road maintenance depot for locomotives and units, which was altered from the original steam buildings, and a two-road refuelling shed tacked onto the side of the maintenance building, specifically for diesels. Two sample sets of observations from the mid-1970s are listed in Table 8.

Class	Locos & DMUs on 17 April 1974	Locos & DMUs on 1 January 1975
08	08129	08016, 08129, 08477, 08524, 08626 & 08676
24	None	24020, 24021, 24024, 24025, 24041 & 24137
25	5238, 25195, 25267 & 25283	25042, 25044, 25050, 25054, 25063, 25110, 25130, 25209, 25235, 25254, 25294, 25297 & 25308
37	None	37173
40	40188	40008, 40010, 40013, 40078, 40091, 40104, 40144, 40181, 40185 & 40196
45	None	45140
47	1834	47214
DMU	81 DMU coaches were present	Not recorded

Table 8: Locos and DMUs present at Newton Heath on two dates in 1974 and 1975.

Below: On 8 June 1977 25166 and 25306 stand outside the south-western end of the diesel maintenance shed. A Class 08 and one of the single-car parcel DMUs allocated to Newton Heath can be seen within the shed and 40153 completes the scene.

Above: Looking from the north-eastern end of the depot on 8 June 1977, 40004 rests at the buffers with 25027 to its right. 25057 can just be made out inside the modern two-road fuelling shed and 40117 is visible on the far right, at the entrance to a modern addition to the maintenance shed.

REDDISH

The depot was a ten-minute walk from Reddish North station which is served by trains from Piccadilly to Rose Hill and New Mills. It was one of the friendliest depots in the North West and I had several relaxed visits there during the 1970s. Reddish depot opened in 1954 as part of the Woodhead Line electrification project and as such was the first "modern image" depot in the UK. Its primary responsibility was the maintenance of the 1500 V DC electric Class 76s used on the line between Manchester and Sheffield, along with the electric multiple units (EMUs) that carried passengers between Manchester and Glossop & Hadfield. In addition, it repaired diesel locomotives in the late 1960s, 1970s and early 1980s. The closure of the Woodhead route in July 1981 led to a big decrease in its work and the subsequent conversion of the lines to Glossop and Hadfield to 25 kV AC power brought about its complete closure in 1983. It was eventually demolished in the 1990s. Two sample lists of locomotives found on shed in the mid-1970s are shown in Table 9. All the images at Reddish were taken on an abysmally gloomy 6 January 1977. On various earlier visits many pictures were taken with my father's ancient Agfa Silette, but none are reproducible!

Class	Locos present on 4 August 1973	Locos present on 1 January 1975
08	3588	None
24 & 25	5029, 5181 & 7654	24023, 25132, 25147 & 25239
40	205, 212, 226 & 229	40004, 40108, 40116 & 40127
47	1787	None
76	26004, 26027, 26028, 26036, 26039, 26046, 26055, 26056, 76003, 76010, 76022, 76037 & 76044	76001, 76003, 76008, 76009, 76010, 76012, 76015, 76018, 76020, 76027, 76040, 76041, 76043, 76044, 76053 & 76057

Table 9: Locos present at Reddish on two dates in 1973 & 1975.

Above: Several withdrawn Class 24s were stored at Reddish in 1977 and this row comprised of 24005, 24024, 24020 and 24021. To their left, the cabs of 76015 and 76033 are visible.

Right: This portrait shows 76047 outside the western end of Reddish depot. This 76 can also be seen in the photograph of the locomotives and EMU that are seen stabled outside the shed buildings.

Right: This external view shows the west end of the four road maintenance shed at Reddish. On the left are the two roads used for inspections and minor repairs, with a correspondingly lower roof as heavy lifting equipment was not needed for these tasks. 40044 and 76047 stand outside this lower shed, while 76007, 76027 and AC electric 304005 rest outside the heavy maintenance depot.

Left: 76046, 76022 and 76051 are seen inside the inspection shed, with one of the DC electric Class 505 EMUs that were used on services to Hadfield and Glossop visible behind.

MANCHESTER STABLING POINTS

BUXTON

The stabling point at Buxton was adjacent to the spa town's passenger terminus and was only a five-minute walk from the station concourse. The shed opened in 1957 and its two roads were primarily designed to service DMUs, although the locomotives used on Peak District stone traffic were also refuelled and serviced there until 1994. This work and the train crew depot were then transferred to Peak Forest. The depot closed in 1997 and was eventually demolished in 2016.

Above: On 7 July 1983, Class 104 vehicles 53491, 59187 & 53430 head away from Buxton station with a service to Manchester Piccadilly. To the side of the passenger train, 37080, 37161 & 37264 are at rest on the depot.

Below: By 1 July 1990, DMUs no longer used Buxton depot. The trio of refurbished Class 37s that were being refuelled and receiving minor attention that day were 37679, 37681 and 37684.

GUIDE BRIDGE

The stabling point at Guide Bridge was accessed via a walkway that began at the end of the station platform. It was responsible for refuelling and stabling the freight locomotives that travelled east on the Woodhead route and west around Manchester and on to Warrington and Liverpool. It was often deserted at the weekend, making a wander round to take photographs relatively easy. The gradual decline of freight traffic at the Manchester end of the Woodhead route, and the closures of Mottram Yard in 1973 and Dewsnap Sidings in 1981, reduced its importance. Most of its traffic was lost in 1981 when the Woodhead route closed and all local freight services were diverted to Ashburys Yard. Sample locomotive lists from two mid-winter dates in 1974 and 1981 are shown in Table 10.

Class	Locos on 28 December 1974	Locos on 1 January 1981
08	08820	08298, 08477, 08599, 08611 & 08820
24	24024, 24040 & 24086	None
25	25141, 25201 & 25297	25143 & 25193
40	40028, 40034, 40105, 40122, 40114, 40119, 40126, 40130 & 40138	40028, 40073, 40076, 40087, 40107, 40120 & 40122
47	47342, 47349, 47364 & 47366	47192, 47228, 47232, 47306, 47344 & 47446
76	76003, 76006, 76007, 76011, 76014, 76023, 76030, 76033, 76036, 76038, 76044, 76048, 76051, 76052 & 76055	76006, 76007, 76009, 76014, 76015, 76026, 76031, 76037 & 76040

Table 10: Locos present at Guide Bridge on two dates in 1974 & 1981.

These three images were taken at Guide Bridge on 11 June 1977 and show a typical array of the motive power that could be found there during the 1970s. Firstly, at the eastern end of the stabling point, an unidentified Class 40 stands alongside 25297, 76041 and 76029. The second image shows 76011, 76014, 76016 and 76012 standing on one of the four electrified tracks at the nine-siding stabling point. Finally, 40020, 40107, 40042 and 40041 rest on one of the two fuelling roads.

‖ **Above:** 76006 is seen through the buffer stops at the western end of Guide Bridge stabling point on 1 January 1981.

‖ **Below:** Also on New Year's Day in 1981 at the western end of Guide Bridge stabling point, from left to right are 76026, 47232, 76007 and 47446.

Above: 40073 is prominent in this general view of Guide Bridge stabling point, again on 1 January 1981. A total of 29 locomotives were "on shed" that day and these are listed in Table 10.

MANCHESTER PICCADILLY

Above: 45106 is seen in the locomotive stabling siding on the eastern side of Piccadilly station on 10 June 1977. The locomotives that arrived on cross country services from the South West and South Wales were the most common users of this siding.

MANCHESTER VICTORIA

Above: One of the most easily observed stabling points in Manchester was this centre road, which lay between Victoria station's Platforms 11 and 12. This was where the locomotives used to bank the heavy freight trains that ascended the steeply-graded Miles Platting Bank would be stabled. On 1 January 1981, 25057 had been assigned this task and awaits its next duty.

Below: Locomotives could be stabled at several spots across the sprawling layout of Manchester Victoria station. One of these was this siding to the east of the Victoria West Junction signal box, where on 11 June 1977 40172 was at rest. It is seen from a Manchester to Holyhead express which I took as far as Warrington, before visiting Arpley Yard stabling point.

CHESTER

The depot at Chester was only a seven-minute walk from the station and there was an excellent vantage point on Hoole Way. This also gave good views of Chester No. 5 signal box prior to its retirement in 1984. The site was extensive, as the panoramic view overleaf shows, with several sheds, many of which had been repurposed from the steam days. The three-road diesel maintenance building had been rebuilt in 1957 and this was a constant until the entire site was redeveloped in the early 2000s. This was deemed necessary because the existing structures were in poor repair and were unsuitable for conversion into a modern servicing facility for the large DMU fleet based in Chester.

Class	Locos
08	08005, 08023, 08070 & 08153
24	24030, 24038, 24045, 24046, 24047, 24060, 24091 & 24134
25	25262
47	47453
DMU	A total of 56 DMU coaches were present

Table 11: Locos present at Chester depot on 26 December 1974.

Above: These two views of the locomotive fuelling point at Chester were taken on 23 April 1976. 24134 and 24063 are joined by 47367, which unusually was still in two-tone green livery at this point. Also present that day at Chester were 25200 and 47449. One constant in all my images of Chester is the three-road servicing shed which opened in 1957; this can be seen to the left of 24134.

Above: On 3 August 1978, from left to right, 08153, 47298 25263 and 25260 stand outside the diesel servicing shed at Chester.

Below: This general view of Chester was taken from Hoole Way on 3 August 1978 and shows the extent of the depot. On the extreme left is the solitary 25043 and to its right is the single-car Class 128 parcels DMU 55993. There were an additional 50 DMU carriages on shed that day, plus the four locomotives shown outside the diesel servicing shed, as shown on the previous photograph.

Above: A bit outside our 20-year time frame, on 22 December 1996, DMUs 101658, 153313 & 101651 fill the erstwhile locomotive servicing shed, which is now only used by DMUs.

CREWE DIESEL DEPOT AND WORKS

In the 1970s THE red letter day in the railway calendar was Crewe Works open day. Enthusiasts from all over the country descended on Crewe and there was standing room only at the end of the station's platforms! Crewe diesel depot had its fair share of trespassers but was usually on high alert as it was only a five-minute walk from the station. My visits to the depot tended to be on quieter days when sneaking round was easier. As for the Works, these were impossible to get into other than on an open day or if you booked on a pre-arranged guided tour. The Works were marvellous, often with over 100 locomotives in various stages of overhaul and repair. Sadly, I was so busy collecting numbers that I have very few pictures of those memorable visits but an example is included below.

Crewe South shed was converted from steam to diesel between 1958 and 1965 and Crewe North shed closed in 1965. Crewe Diesel, to the south of the station, then became the primary depot in Crewe and the last steam locomotives to use it were withdrawn in 1967. As sectorisation came along, the diesel depot was assigned to Railfreight Distribution and then taken over by EWS in 1992. With the loss of Royal Mail trains, the depot closed in 2004 but has since seen a rebirth as the main base for the LNWR Railway Heritage Company.

Class	Locos on 26 December 1974	Locos on 10 July 1978
08	08036, 08055, 08068, 08220, 08222, 08395, 08416, 08631, 08633, 08634 & 08694	08080, 08222, 08289, 08382, 08737 & 08802
20	20057	None
24	24031, 24032, 24048, 24049, 24053, 24054, 24076, 24078, 24081, 24083, 24084, 24087, 24092, 24133 & 24136	24073, 24087 & 24133
25	25134, 25139, 25162, 25196, 25289 & 25290	25043, 25063, 25130, 25161, 25185, 25192 & 25211
31	None	31302
40	40069, 40125 & 40177	40013, 40055, 40087, 40128, 40144, 40151, 40170 & 40174
47	47182, 47188, 47191, 47193, 47197, 47228, 47264, 47341, 47344, 47357, 47442, 47450, 47451, 47456, 47515 & 47536	47034, 47194, 47350, 47352 & 47490
50	50017, 50029, 50034, 50045 & 50047	None
81–87	83012, 86015 & 87026	84009, 85032, 85036, 86018, 86231, 86254, 87011 & 87026

Table 12: Locos present at Crewe Diesel on two days in 1974 and 1978.

Left, top & above: On 10 July 1978 the diesel depot at Crewe held 38 diesel and electric locomotives, which include those shown on these three images. 40151 is undergoing tests in the holding sidings outside the main shed. 24073 is stabled next to withdrawn classmates 24087 & 24133 and 47490 & 40087 are seen in the locomotive holding sidings. A full list of the locomotives present that day is given in Table 12.

Class	Locos
08	3031, 3113, 3292, 3970 & 3984
40	200, 223, 242, 250, 251, 280, 283, 288, 309, 310, 314, 316, 317, 325, 352, 354, 359, 375, 391 & 392
47	1102, 1500, 1502, 1503, 1527, 1554, 1564, 1568, 1569, 1589, 1612, 1620, 1625, 1643, 1663, 1681, 1690, 1695, 1727, 1751, 1752, 1761, 1771, 1776, 1818, 1822, 1826, 1846, 1872, 1886, 1911, 1916, 1930, 1933, 1951, 1960, 1968, 1992, 1996 & 1997
50	410, 420, 431, 436, 439 & 440
81–86	E3016, E3021, E3058, E3068, E3102, E3106, E3109, E3120, E3145, E3146, E3147, E3151, E3163, E3165, E3166, E3171, E3175, E3177, E3193, 81019, 85003, 86008, 86013, 86202, 86206, 86210 & 86217
87	87001, 87006, 87007, 87008, 87009, 87011, 87012, 87013, 87014, 87015, 87016, 87017, 87018, 87020 & 87021

Table 13: Locos present at Crewe Works on 15 August 1973. The large number of Class 87s was because they were under construction at Crewe at the time.

Above: On 5 August 1978, on my way from Colwyn Bay to Derby Works open day, a change of trains at Crewe was necessary and this view was grabbed from the end of the platform. 40134 sits alongside 47182, 47473 and at least two other 47s, with the main shed just visible above the line-up.

Right: Reviewing my shots of Crewe Works it looks as if I got a bit over excited, as all but this one are blurred – no doubt a result of rushing round to collect as many numbers as possible! On 6 August 1975, 47347 stands at the No. 2 locomotive testing station in what looks like ex-works condition.

THE NORTH EAST

ASHINGTON

Above: As it wasn't owned or operated by BR, the National Coal Board's (NCB) locomotive depot at Ashington was never represented in the Ian Allan Locoshed Directory, upon which this album is loosely based, but it had an allocation of ex-BR Class 14 0-6-0s for many years. In 1978, 11 of the Class were allocated to the colliery (D9500, D9508, D9511, D9514, D9517–18, D9521, D9527–28, D9531 & D9536). This view, taken on 12 August 1986, shows two other Class 14s that had been transferred to Ashington from Backworth Colliery when it closed a couple of years earlier. No. 507 is the former D9525 and No. 38 is the former D9513.

BLYTH CAMBOIS

The diesel depot at Blyth Cambois opened in 1968 and replaced the depots at Percy Main, Blyth South and Blyth North which all became surplus to requirement in 1967 when steam finished in the North East. It was one of the most challenging depots to visit when using public transport and the Locoshed Directory has reminded me that after catching a bus from Newcastle to Blyth Ferry, one had to catch the ferry across to the north bank of the harbour and then walk to the depot, which I did in 1974. The journey time to reach this outpost was 90 minutes each way from Newcastle! The depot handled 30 coal diagrams per day back in the mid-1970s, but this had reduced to 20 diagrams by the 1980s when I found myself working in the nearby

Below: On 28 December 1988 the depot was full, with nine Class 56s and two Class 08s. Visible in this view, which was taken from the south, from left to right are 56130, 56115 & 56113 and 37040.

Ashington Hospital for six months. Hence most of my images at the depot were taken during that time. As coal mining collapsed in the North East at the end of the 1980s, the depot's work disappeared and so it closed in 1994 and was demolished shortly thereafter.

Right: Taken at the north end of the depot on 31 October 1987, this view shows the short siding where the two Class 08s were usually parked. 08888 and 08442 were resident that day, along with 56116 which is visible in the distance. My notes record that 56112, 56134, 56121 and 56118 were also on shed that day.

Above: 37059 and 37242 undergo minor repairs in the small maintenance shed at Cambois on 17 April 1987.

Right: On 20 April 1988, five Class 56s in Large Logo livery line up along the eastern edge of the shed, some of which have been given names reflecting the area's industry. The locos visible are 56134 "Blyth Power", 56124 "Blue Circle Cement", 56131 "Ellington Colliery", 56130 "Wardley Opencast" and 56116.

GATESHEAD

The steam depot at Gateshead was gradually converted to a diesel depot between 1960 and 1965. In its heyday, it had an allocation of over 200 locomotives and it remained active until its closure in 1994. A housing estate has since been built on the land formerly occupied by the depot. Gateshead was a 15-minute walk from Newcastle Central station and was one of the most difficult depots to get round because the main office had a bird's eye view of the main approach. I didn't manage to get inside the shed until 1983 when a local enthusiast showed me the back way in. This was accessed from a small lane that passed under the eastern approach track to the King Edward Bridge! Just like Bristol Bath Road, the best way in was from the back!

Class	Locos on 12 August 1975	Locos on 7 July 1978	Locos on Christmas Day 1987
03	03064, 03102, 03108 & 03170	03056 & 03069	03063, 03066, 03094 & 03371
08	08058, 08325 & 08516	08001, 08116, 08148, 08445, 08516 & 08747	08254, 08421, 08441, 08507, 08512, 08515, 08521, 08544, 08577, 08608, 08671 & 08797
31	31236 & 31316	31186, 31406 & 31418	31141, 31196, 31426, 31427, 31428 & 31462
37	37082	37001, 37010, 37074 & 37097	37046, 37059, 37098, 37244, 37303 & 37512
40	40096, 40145, 40147, & 40184	40032, 40057, 40071, 40074 & 40086	None (all but 40122 had been withdrawn by 1987)
46	46036, 46037, 46042, 46046 & 46053	46034, 46041, 46049, 46051, 46054 & 46056	None (all withdrawn by 1987)
47	47410, 47419, 47435 & 47461	47129, 47192, 47293, 47420, 47425, 47429 & 47520	47125, 47146, 47195, 47330, 47401, 47407, 47413, 47418, 47420, 47425, 47443, 47523, 47542, 47566, 47619, 47634 & 47655
55	55005	55005	None (all withdrawn by 1987)
56	None	None	56113, 56115, 56116, 56117, 56119, 56123, 56125, 56127, 56128, 56129, 56133 & 56135

Table 14: Locos present at Gateshead on three dates in 1975, 1978 and 1987.

Below: This winter view was taken on 14 January 1983, which was when I was first shown how to access the depot from the rear. 40044 and 46025 are stabled among other Type 4s at the back of the depot.

These three images, which were taken on 7 July 1978, don't tell the full story of my visit to Gateshead. As I approached the depot I was accosted by the foreman and promptly thrown out. I managed to take the picture of 37097 while approaching the entrance to the shed as I apologised profusely and beat a hasty retreat.

I turned to photograph 37010 and also captured 40071 & 40032 in the distance and 03069, 08445 & 46034 behind the 37. Having failed to get into the depot, I found a patch of waste ground to the south of the depot avoiding line and from there I took the picture of the two-road fuelling and inspection shed that hosted 46056, 40074 and 47293.

Above: An unusual image in that it was taken using a telephoto lens inside the main building at Gateshead. On 5 October 1986, from left to right are 47410, 03094, 03063, an unidentified 08, 56081 and 47232.

Above: This was an unusual sight on 15 May 1987, because by then Class 56s had taken over from Class 37s on most of the coal workings in the North East and some of the newer and more powerful 56s that Gateshead looked after would usually be present. From left to right at the refuelling shed are 37226, 37177, 37074, 37059 and 37070.

Above: These two pictures, which were taken inside the main maintenance shed on 28 June 1987, illustrate how the majority of the work undertaken at the time was on Classes 47 and 56. In the wide angle view 47406 & 47130 stand alongside 56117 & 56121, whilst the nose of 56123 is seen on the left edge of the picture. The second image shows 47406 from a different angle and 56119 & 56113 to its right.

Above: The roads inside Gateshead's maintenance shed were busy when this view was captured on 15 October 1986. 56126 and 56135 can be seen on the left, with 47410 and two of the depot's remaining allocation of Class 03 shunters in the centre – 03094 and 03063. On the right, a member of staff is kneeling down in front of 47232 with 47665 visible just behind it.

Above: On Christmas Day in 1987 I paid an after-lunch visit to Gateshead. There was a solitary security guard on duty at the east end of the depot and I spied him in his office eating mince pies. Other than that there was not a soul to be seen anywhere around the depot area, so I was able to capture 37059 in the maintenance shed along with 37512 and 47542. The other locos on shed that day are listed above in Table 14.

Above: The doors to Roads 1, 2 and 3 at the east end of the nine-road maintenance shed are open on 15 May 1989, when 47634 "Henry Ford" was found at the refuelling point.

Above: Also on 14 May 1989, the fuelling point was captured on film, where 31264, 47411 and 08489 were present.

Above: This was one of the last images I took of Gateshead before moving away from the North East. The date was 10 September 1989 and by then the depot was already looking forlorn. Only part of the maintenance facility was still in use and the number of locomotives using the depot was significantly reduced. From left to right in this view are 31249, 47526 (partially hidden), 47515, 47442, 47475 behind the fuel oil tank, 08802, an unidentified 37, 08489 with another 08 and finally 47626. The maintenance buildings at this time were often nearly empty, reflecting the reduced workload after responsibility for the Class 56 fleet had been transferred to Toton in late 1987 and the cessation of all maintenance at Gateshead in 1988.

TYNE YARD

Several major stabling points were linked to Gateshead, most notable amongst them were Tyne Yard and Sunderland South Dock. Tyne Yard servicing point opened alongside the new Tyne Yard in 1963 and serviced the freight locomotives passing through the hump yard. Although traffic fell steadily, the depot remained active because in 1994 it took over the work undertaken by the stabling points at Blyth and Sunderland, both of which closed that year. The buildings were extended in the late 1990s and today there is a four-road maintenance shed for locomotives and DMUs. The bridge to the north of Tyne Yard, from which the stabling point was visible, could be reached by the bus service to nearby Kibblesworth. On a good day, one was able to wander down the drive to the depot and record most of the engines on site.

Above: The south end of the original Tyne Yard servicing depot is seen on 23 November 1984. 46035 is parked outside the main building which has a single through track for wagon maintenance and a single dead end track for locomotive fuelling and inspection. Also stabled on shed that day were 37041, 37061, 37078, 37169, 37199 and 37283.

Above: Standing at Tyne Yard's fuelling road on 2 June 1988 are 47307 and 31278. The 31 had finished refuelling and left shortly after this view was captured to work 9N05, a trip freight to Berwick-upon-Tweed. The Railfreight-liveried 37 was an unusual sight in that it was hauling the daily Healey Mills to Mossend Speedlink Coal service and had to call at Tyne Yard to "knock out" four FPA container wagons which had hot boxes and needed to be repaired.

Above: On 29 October 1988 the stabling sidings to the south of Tyne Yard depot contain 31278, 37046 and 47306, plus half a dozen other locomotives, the numbers of which I didn't record.

Above: This close-up at the north end of the shed at Tyne Yard shows 37071 on 20 January 1990, with the through track used for wagon maintenance to its right.

SUNDERLAND SOUTH DOCK

When steam finished at Sunderland's South Dock depot in July 1967, its roundhouse was demolished but the four-road steam shed was retained as a diesel depot. Virtually no alterations were made and the funnels on the roof, which had been installed to catch rising steam, remained in place throughout the nearly 20 years it operated as a diesel depot! It was a 20-minute walk from Sunderland station and my recollection is that the depot's staff were always friendly to visiting spotters and that it was easy to visit.

Class	Locos
08	08081, 08116 & 08147
37	37028, 37048, 37032, 37083 & 37195

Table 15: Locos present at Sunderland on 10 August 1976.

Left & below: Two views of Sunderland Depot on 19 April 1987, which was well into the Class 56 era. Inside the shed, 56131 is seen underneath the steam era funnels that were never removed when steam finished in 1967; these look somewhat incongruous still hanging there in 1989. The outside view shows the loco line up which from left to right consists of 56119 with 56129 behind, 56125 with 56131 behind, 56112 with 56123 behind and 56122 in the shadows. To the right of the shed is 08442 with two guards vans.

Below: This view is especially poignant as it was taken on Christmas Eve 1988 when we were invited for sherry with the late railway photographer I S Carr. It was a memorable day as my son Jonathan was just four days old and was presented with a card by Ian. Inside was a £5 note and a message which read "To Jonathan Railroad Rhodes, £5 towards your first camera". Enroute to Ian's, we popped into South Dock to find 56129 at the new fuelling point which had been built earlier that year. To its left, four classmates and an 08 are also at rest ahead of the Christmas break.

Above: On 25 September 1985 I visited Simonside Wagon Works, which was located on the Tyne Dock branch. Chatting to the foreman, pictured on the right in this view, I discovered that it had been designated as a new stabling point for two shunting locomotives. 03066 is pictured here and 08442 was behind the camera. Both locomotives were about to be locked in the shed for the night to prevent vandalism and would be let out at 07.30 the next morning.

Right: One far flung stabling point for Gateshead was the goods yard at Berwick-upon-Tweed, just south of the Royal Border Bridge. This was the scene on 16 July 1984 when 03063 was found stabled there.

THORNABY

The depot at Thornaby was a 15-minute walk from the station and I always found it friendly during my visits in the 1970s and 1980s. Indeed, during the 1980s I was fortunate to make some official visits and had access to the lighting masts which could be used as vantage points to take pictures. The depot was built as a steam shed in 1958 but it soon became clear that it would have to be slightly adapted for diesels. The last steam allocation left in 1965. Thornaby was one of the largest depots on the network, with 19 tracks to the various sheds and a roundhouse which was used during the diesel era, albeit mainly for wagon repairs. By comparison, the depot at Toton had just 16 tracks into the engine shed. The stabling points linked to Thornaby in the 1970s were Hartlepool, which had been closed by the time I visited the town, and Tees Yard where the shunting locomotives that worked in the double hump yard were stabled at weekends. The depot remained busy in the 1980s and 1990s, but as DB Cargo moved the maintenance of its fleet to Toton, Thornaby declined and was closed in 2007, being demolished in 2011. Table 16 shows sample lists of the locomotives found there during the mid 1970s.

Class	Locos on 30 May 1974	Locos on 12 August 1975	Locos on 7 July 1978
03	03067, 03099, 03107 & 03154	03010, 03153 & 03171	03075
08	08174, 08215 & 08770	08310, 08389, 08770 & 08774	08044, 08212, 08215, 08373, 08502 & 08632
31	31130, 31132, 31137, 31152, 31297 & 31300	31130, 31143, 31152, 31173, 31278, 31290 & 31292	31130, 31139, 31282 & 31292
37	37007, 37013, 37067, 37094, 37168, 37198 & 37250	37001, 37007, 37036, 37048, 37072, 37084, 37143, 37160, 37161, 37165, 37195 & 37198	37002, 37003, 37005, 37006, 37015, 37069, 37077, 37081, 37161 & 37219
40	None	40151	40194
46	None	46050	None
47	47286 & 47290	47288, 47360 & 47445	47287, 47291 & 47459

Table 16: Locos present at Thornaby on three dates during the 1970s.

Below & right: These two views of a trio of Thornaby 37s were captured on 7 July 1978 when I called in while on my way to Scotland. 37003, 37005 & 37069 are visible from the eastern end of the depot and from inside the shed.

Right: On 7 July 1978 37002 is seen in the main maintenance building raised up on trackside jacks, as it undergoes a bogie change.

Above: These next two photos were taken on my 7 July 1978 visit to Thornaby. From left to right are 31282 with an unidentified Class 47s behind it, 31130, 31292 and 37081. In 1978 the doors to the depot had illuminated displays above them advising whether to proceed or wait. These had been replaced by simple track numbers by the 1980s.

Above: With the lighting masts of the Up Hump Yard at Tees visible in the background, 08502 has come onto shed for refuelling. The prefabricated concrete shelter at the refuelling point is very similar to those at other north-eastern depots such as Gateshead. A full list of the locomotives on the depot that day can be seen in Table 16.

Right: On 24 November 1984, the line up at the western end of maintenance tracks 6–11 is, from left to right, 47330, then a row of four Class 31, 31281, 31210, 31138 & 31319, followed by 31324 and 37195 on separate roads.

Above: Roads 15–19 at Thornaby were for DMUs and various members of the local Metro-Cammell fleet are seen stabled on these on 24 November 1984. At night the sidings numbered 18 & 19 were used for carriage cleaning. During the day when the DMUs were out on the Saltburn, Newcastle and Bishop Auckland services, all five tracks shown here were commandeered by the Carriage & Wagon Department for wagon repairs. Then by 15.30 each day the wagons had to be removed and either returned to service or stabled in the old ash pits overnight. One former depot driver described this daily routine as a "right pain in the...."! By the 1990s, the DMUs were cleaned at Middlesborough and refuelled at Gateshead.

Above: The roads numbered 9 to 14 at the depot were allocated for minor inspections and refuelling. By the time this image was taken on 21 February 1987, siding numbers 13 and 14 had been taken over by the Carriage & Wagon Department for wagon repairs. 37502 and 37511 are seen here in the refuelling area on Roads 9 to 10.

Above: No series of diesel images at Thornaby would be complete without mention of the Class 20 fleet that was based there between 1987 and 1992. Members of the class rendered surplus to requirement elsewhere (predominantly Scotland) were transferred to Thornaby which had a fleet of 12 locomotives to handle traffic on the Redmire and Boulby branches. On 21 February 1987, 20172, 20070, 20175 & 20028 line up on the track between Roads 8 and 9 at the western side of the depot. Note the kingfishers that have been applied to the sides of 20172 and 20070; this was the icon that the depot's staff applied to locomotives to mark them out as being allocated to Thornaby. Also present are 31238, 08506 and 08504.

Above: Inside the heavy maintenance area on 21 February 1987 was the unnumbered 37501 in light blue. Thornaby were famous for embellishing their locomotives and perhaps this unique paint scheme was the most striking. 37259 is behind the celebrity locomotive.

Above: This interior view shows Roads 4–7 of the heavy maintenance shed on 21 February 1987. 45033 and 08872 stand on Road 5, while Road 6 is occupied by a BDA wagon undergoing major repairs. The use of the heavy maintenance area to deal with wagons as well as locomotives became more commonplace in the 1980s. To the right of the wagon are 47305 and 37503 on Road 7. The image of 37501 pictures it on the last of the heavy maintenance tracks, Row 8.

Below: This view of Thornaby was taken from the eastern end of the complex on 21 February 1987. On the left is Road 1 which was used for stabling VDA vans. Normally two vans arrived each day with supplies, one from Crewe and one from Doncaster. On this day there were four vans and a fuel oil tank on the track, as well as 08774. The next two sidings, Nos. 2 & 3, lead to the small maintenance shed for shunting engines and they contain 08334, 08519, 08582 and 08575 on Road 2, with 08906 & 08502 and 45070 on Road 3. Next are the heavy maintenance Roads, Nos. 4 to 8, outside of which are 31138, 31306, 37198 and 37193. Roads 9 to 12 are for refuelling and inspections. Inside the building on Roads 9 and 10 are 37068 and 37502 whilst 47290 stands outside on Road 10. I failed to record the number of the 31 on Road 11 or the DMU inside the shed on Road 12. By 1987, the track at the eastern end of Roads 13 and 14 was being modified for use by the Carriage & Wagon Department.

Above: I have included this image because it shows a facet of Thornaby that I think was almost unique amongst diesel depots at the time. To the north of the 19 shed roads were further holding sidings and on 21 February 1987, from left to right these contain 47408, 08879, 45124 and 45110. Wandering between them are three "shed bashers" and as I recall, some of the foremen at Thornaby would provide visitors with yellow vests and even accompany them. My visit this day was sanctioned by the person in charge who simply said "Just be careful as you go round and let me know when you're leaving"!

Above: On 4 June 1993, this view was possible because of the construction of a new access road across the middle of Tees Yard to allow development of the land formerly occupied by the down sorting sidings. There are 15 locomotives stored in the foreground of the picture, with the nearest row containing 08295, 20094, 20096, 20144, 20008, 20214 and 20046. The expanse of the 19 shed roads and the ash pits to the right are all included in what is my favourite panorama of the depot. Sadly, even though it was June, the weather was poor!

Above: Occupying the same roads that 37003, 37005 & 37069 are standing on in the earlier July 1978 view from inside the shed, are 60030, 60038 and some wagons under repair. 60007 and a Class 37 can also be seen parked outside.

Below: This final image of Thornaby was taken on 31 August 1994. It was captured from the new road across the yard during a one-week trip back to the UK from Australia to look at consultant jobs. During the era of sectorisation, Railfreight Metals were the sector in charge of the depot. From left to right, the locomotives nearest the camera at the end of each row are 47095, 56134, 47396, 56081, 56089 and 60090.

DARLINGTON

A ten-minute walk from the station, the DMU depot at Darlington was always fairly easy to look round, but rarely held more than a couple of main line locomotives. BR's North Eastern Region had opened a purpose built depot for DMUs to the north of Darlington station on the west of the ECML in 1957. As well as DMUs, it also had a small allocation of shunting locomotives which worked around Darlington and at Shildon Wagon Works. The depot closed in 1984 when its shunters and DMUs were all reallocated to Thornaby. It was demolished shortly after closure and the land that it formerly occupied is now largely woodland.

A typical haul at the depot in the mid 1970s is shown in Table 17, although it should be noted that four of the locomotives were stabled on the east side of the ECML in Croft Sidings.

Class	Locos
08	08063 & 08167
31	31290
37	37010, 37032, 37077 & 37160

Table 17: Locos present at Darlington on 10 August 1976.

Above: Taken on 11 February 1984, this view of Darlington depot used a 500mm mirror lens to zoom in from the footbridge over the ECML, which is to the north of Darlington station. Tucked away to the left is a pair of 31s on the refuelling road whilst the rest of the depot is full of the Metro-Cammell DMUs used on the services to Bishop Auckland and Saltburn. These were transferred to Thornaby later that year.

YORK

The diesel depot at York was a 10-minute walk from the station and I found it to be fairly welcoming and easy to look round. There were two steam depots at York, South and North, and it was York North that became the diesel depot. The six-track steam shed, which was built in 1957, became the maintenance depot for diesels and this survived until 1982 when York was downgraded to a stabling point. The stabling point itself closed in 1991 and the entire site is now part of the National Railway Museum. Locomotives stabled in York station, as well as Scarborough where York-allocated shunting locomotives would be found. A typical line up in the depot during the early 1970s is summarised in Table 18.

Class	Locos
03	2090, 2150 & 2172
08	3076
31	5520, 5521, 5523, 5538, 5559, 5585, 5587, 5588 & 5840
40	243, 250, 259, 261, 270 & 283
44–46	44 & 90
47	1107
55	9008 & 9011

Table 18: Locos present at York on 26 April 1973.

Above: 37015 and 40150 are stabled in the sidings between the diesel maintenance depot and the ECML at York on 24 August 1974. Also on shed that day were 03172, 08707, 31108, 31146, 31148, 31179, 31304, 40047, 40050, 40057, 40070, 40074, 40083, 40183 , 40192, 47003, 47418, 47454, 47467, 47519, 47526 and 47554.

Above: This is the first of five views taken at York depot on 9 June 1977, showing 40052 and 55012 inside the four-track heavy maintenance shed.

Above left, left & below: These three images show the northern end of the 1957-built six-track shed. 47521 and 40081 can be seen in each of the photographs, two of which also illustrate 47524 on the left. The two shorter sidings on the right of the general view (the one taken from further back) make up Roads 5 and 6 of the servicing shed and were often empty during my visits.

Above: On 9 June 1977 the stabling sidings are full at York with 31325, 31312, 31272 and 31284 lined up beside a fifth unidentified Class 31. Also present on the depot that day, but not illustrated in the five images, were 03172, 08525, 25159, 31127, 31264, 37003 ,37070, 40049, 40064, 40086, 46004, 47036, 47460, 47471 and 47526.

Right: Deltics 55013 "THE BLACK WATCH" and 55002 "THE KING'S OWN YORKSHIRE LIGHT INFANTRY" undergo maintenance inside York depot on 2 January 1980. These two locomotives, along with 11 other stablemates, were allocated to York for the last 18 months of their working lives. For the last six months of the Deltics' working lives another four locomotives were also allocated to York.

Left: There are plenty of brake blocks to spare at York on 2 January 1980, separating 08062 from 40085 and 40067 inside the heavy maintenance shed.

Above: York-allocated 03089 undergoes major repairs at its home depot on 2 January 1980. The small fleet of Class 03s that were allocated to York were used on trip workings to the nearby Rowntree factory and on station pilot duties at Scarborough.

Below: This final view of York taken on 2 January 1980 shows 47522 and 47401 standing alongside 55017 at the north end of the maintenance building. The fourth road is occupied by a DMU power car that is being repaired at the depot.

HULL BOTANIC GARDENS

The depot was a 15-minute walk from Hull Paragon station and several visits were made during the 1970s. It opened in 1959 and was designed mainly to service the DMUs that entered service on the majority of the local passenger services at the time. As the importance of the port in Hull diminished, so did the facilities that serviced steam locomotives and their diesel replacements on the freight traffic in the area. From 1970, when Hull Dairycoates depot closed, Botanic Gardens became the main diesel servicing shed for the whole area. Freight traffic virtually evaporated from Hull when the docks initially refused to containerise, giving Immingham on the south bank of the Humber the opportunity to become the premier port on the Humber. Consequently, Botanic Gardens was downgraded and in 1987 it was reclassified as a refuelling point. It could have been closed altogether but was rebuilt (albeit on a much smaller scale) in the early 2000s to act as DMU servicing point. During the 1970s there were several stabling points linked to the depot including Hessle Yard, Hull Docks and Goole. The largest of these was at Goole and this often held half a dozen locomotives at the weekend.

Above: In this general view of the sidings at Goole Docks that was taken on 3 January 1989, the stabling point and crew signing on building are on the left, with 08583 and 37255 in attendance.

Above: On 7 August 1975, 31280 stands in the stabling sidings at Hull Botanic Gardens with 03137 visible in the distance. Also present on the depot that day were a couple of dozen DMU carriages, 03073, 03157, 08063, 08064, 08165, 08248, 08514, 20058, 20132, 20200 & 20209, 37246 and 47216.

Above: On a very gloomy 31 December 1974, 37112 is seen on the depot at Botanic Gardens. Behind the locomotive is Botanic Gardens signal box with Hull Royal Infirmary on the right. To think that nearly 40 years later in 2012, I would end up doing surgical clinics as a consultant there for six months! Also present that day were 03073, 03158, 08004, 08064, 08164, 08253, 08514, 08777, 20022, 20056, 20119, 20127, 37209, 40155 and 47220.

LEEDS HOLBECK

The depot at Holbeck was a 20-minute walk from Leeds City station and was one which I was thrown out of every time I tried to visit! I did manage to record the locomotives on shed under the cover of darkness in 1974 however, and observed the locomotives shown in Table 19. Steam and diesel coexisted at Holbeck until 1967, after which large numbers of diesels used the old steam turntable and steam workshops. A two-road refuelling and inspection shed was added for diesels in the late 1960s. With the introduction of HSTs on passenger services to London and on the cross-country routes, and the drop in freight traffic, the depot lost its allocation in the late 1980s and Neville Hill took over as the main depot for the Leeds area. The site at Holbeck is still used today by Network Rail and RTS Infrastructure.

Class	Locos
08	08309 & 08766
25	5176
31	31156, 31281, 31310 & 31409
45–46	19, 21, 78, 91, 125, 129 & 136
47	1774, 47050, 47460 & 47528
55	55007

Table 19: Locos present at Holbeck on 18 April 1974.

Below: This is the only photograph I ever managed to take at Leeds Holbeck depot. On 9 June 1977, 40161 stands in front of 08517 and 45032. They were the only numbers I managed to record before the shed foreman escorted me from the premises. Every cloud has a silver lining though, as I then called in at the newly built Dragonara Hotel and was allowed onto the roof which afforded spectacular views over Leeds City station.

KNOTTINGLEY

The depot is just a ten-minute walk from Knottingley station and had the advantage that most locomotives "on shed" could be seen from the high-level approach road, meaning the need to trespass was diminished! Opened in 1967 as a purpose-built diesel depot, it served traffic to the Calder Valley power stations for over five decades. The collapse of coal traffic, first from the Yorkshire Coalfield and then from Immingham Docks could have led to its closure. The depot however has recently been taken over by Riviera Trains and so it plays host to the company's coaches and a small number of locomotives. A typical line up at the depot in the mid-1970s, before the introduction of Class 5 motive power, is shown in Table 20.

Class	Locos
08	08206, 08305 & 08309
47	47277, 47301, 47302, 47308, 47309, 47310, 47319, 47371, 47372, 47373 & 47375

Table 20: Locos present at Knottingley on 28 December 1974.

Right: This classic view of Knottingley was taken from the elevated approach road on 12 July 1984 and shows the cooling towers of Ferrybridge Power Station in the background. The depot is unusually full, as this was in the middle of the 1984 Miners' Strike. From left to right are 56124, 56073, 56011, 56023, 56112, 56086 and 08309.

Left, above & right: These three images were taken during an official visit to the depot on 9 May 1989. At this stage, Knottingley was responsible for 22 Class 56s and two Class 08s. Ten of the 56s and both 08s are shown here but to my shame I did not record all their numbers because I was too busy climbing the lighting mast (under supervision) and chatting to the depot foreman. The locos visible include 56093, 56047, 56075 and 08309. The final image shows the facilities inside the refuelling shed which houses the second to fourth roads (from the left) that are visible on the aerial shot.

HEALEY MILLS

Healey Mills was always a struggle to get to and involved a 30-minute bus ride from Wakefield to Ossett. The journey was worth it just for the excitement of walking down the steep hill from Ossett with the vast expanse of Healey Mills Marshalling Yard stretching as far as the eye could see. The depot was almost impossible to get round because it was accessed by a railway employee footbridge, which unlike the one at Cardiff Canton, was heavily policed! The diesel depot at Healey Mills opened in 1966, three years after the neighbouring marshalling yard was commissioned. This was because initially most freight services at

Healey Mills were steam hauled. The hump at Healey Mills closed in 1984 as a direct result of the Miners' strike and the dramatic drop in coal traffic in Yorkshire. The main diesel depot fell into disuse in 1988. There was a brief renaissance when Trainload Petroleum opened a single track servicing depot at Healey Mills in 1993, but this closed in 1999. The whole complex was razed to the ground in 2016 and of all the former modernisation plan hump yards, Healey Mills is now the most desolate, with nature taking over the entire site. Two typical line ups at Healey Mills from the mid-1970s are shown in Table 21.

Class	Locos on 1 June 1974	Locos on 9 August 1975
03	03166	03166
08	08057, 08162, 08163, 08306, 08307, 08308 & 08372	08056, 08098, 08163, 08243, 08295, 08307, 08311 & 08706
31	31155 & 31319	31417
37	37021, 37246 & 37251	37021, 37096, 37245 & 37246
40	40005, 40006, 40007, 40012, 40037, 40039, 40040, 40046, 40049, 40056, 40068, 40102, 40134, 40169 & 40187	40006, 40026, 40037, 40039, 40046, 40048, 40049, 40148, 40192 & 40198
45	45013	None
47	None	47302

Table 21: Locos present at Healey Mills on two dates in 1974 and 1975.

Above: During an official visit on 20 May 1985, sadly just a few months after the hump had closed at Healey Mills, I finally got access to the maintenance depot. Inside was a solitary 25200.

Left: This view, taken on 25 May 1974, has been selected because it shows the two main diesel depot buildings at Healey Mills. To the right of 31310, which is coming on shed, are the maintenance building and to its right and a fair way back, the refuelling and inspection shed. The business of Healey Mills can be seen from the two Class 08s and Class 25 next to the three-aspect colour light signal on the left. To the right of 31310 are members of Classes 08, 31, 37 and 40, whilst on the far right in the refuelling shed is another Class 40. Present on shed that day were 03047, 08226, 08243, 08307, 08308, 08773, 25133, 31319, 31410, 37160, 37240, 37246, 40006, 40040, 40086, 40194 and finally 46046.

Above: On 11 August 1993, the locomotives lined up outside the now disused maintenance depot are 47213 (left), 08525, 08579, 08305, 08659 and 47340 behind the shunters.

Above: On the left is Healey Mills' former maintenance shed. Behind it and to the right is the brand-new Trainload Petroleum Diesel Servicing Point. Stabled in the sidings which were previously used for re-crewing through freights at Healey Mills are 31110 and 56090.

DONCASTER

Doncaster shed was a 20-minuite walk from the station and annoyingly was only partially visible from passing trains on the ECML. It was recorded in my notes as neither difficult nor easy to "bunk" and I visited many times during the 1970s and 1980s. The steam depot at Doncaster was gradually converted for use as a diesel depot in the early 1960s, with the main diesel maintenance depot constructed in 1964. This six-track new build was supplemented by the use of six further tracks from the former steam shed on the west of the complex. The steam buildings over these tracks were demolished in the early 1980s, but the lines continued to be used right until the end of the depot's life in 2014, when it was demolished to make way for a new Hitachi electric unit depot. This now covers all the ground that the former diesel depot occupied, as well as a significant tract of land that was part of the former "Up" Hump Yard. Three samples of the varied motive power that could be found on the depot during the mid-1970s are given in Table 22.

Class	Locos on 29 May 1974	Locos on 27 July 1974	Locos on 7 January 1977
03	2173, 03151, 03152 & 03174	03371	None
08	3037, 3069, 3075, 3078, 08101 & 08184	3037, 3069, 08101, 08146, 08373, 08417, 08435 & 08607	08002, 08042, 08131, 08136, 08241, 08444, 08516 & 08553
20	20023 & 20209	None	20028
24	None	None	24097, 24099, 24125, 24126 & 24127
31	31242	31106, 31113, 31155, 31232, 31238, 31242, 31263 & 31296	31179, 31209, 31245 & 31307
37	37021, 37037 37049 & 37167	37008, 37028, 37065, & 37098	37013, 37030 & 37201
40	40078	40085	40037 & 40103
45–46	None	24 & 46045	45006
47	47100, 47/102, 47160, 47177, 47209, 47401, 47409, 47410 & 47414	47042, 47102, 47172, 47176, 47216 & 47430	47040, 47115, 47183, 47184, 47215, 47263, 47311 & 47370
55	55006	None	55005

Table 22: Locos present at Doncaster on three dates during the mid-1970s.

Above: 31232 stands at the south end of the old steam shed at Doncaster Depot on 27 July 1974. In the background a former steam tender is visible; this had been repurposed as an independent snow plough and given the number DE330963. The other locos present at the depot that day are listed in Table 22.

Above: The next three views were all taken on 7 January 1977. The first shows 45006 "HONOURABLE ARTILLERY COMPANY" at the north end of Doncaster shed with 55005 and 55018 behind. The locomotives in the third column of Table 22 were also recorded on the depot that day.

Above: The five Class 24s listed in Table 24 had all been moved to Doncaster after being withdrawn from service in Scotland during 1976. They were awaiting the scrap man in the nearby BREL Doncaster Works and would all be disposed of before the end of 1977.

Above: Taken into the low winter sun, this image shows the new diesel shed on the left with a variety of diesels parked outside. To the right of these are the six tracks that were used to store the locomotives and wagons under repair and these are covered by what remains of the old steam shed.

Below: This similar view from the north of Doncaster shed was taken on 2 July 1985 and shows that the old steam shed has now been demolished, although the tracks are still being used to stable main line locos. On the far left, with its rear wall facing the photographer, is the taller two track heavy maintenance shed for diesels. Next to these are the four roads to the light maintenance and refuelling building. Three Class 08s can be seen on the second track of this part of the depot, whilst in contrast the uncovered stabling area is filled with a variety of freight locomotives.

DONCASTER WORKS

Just a ten-minute walk from Doncaster station, Doncaster Works was like all of the BR Engineering Ltd (BREL) workshops, impossible to bunk! With the workshops gated and security tight, the only way to visit was during an open day or by writing to request an official permit. In the 1970s however, open days were frequent, at least one per year, and permits were obtained relatively easily. My first visit to Doncaster Works was during the open day of 27 July 1974, when the locomotives listed in Table 23 were noted. The Works had begun building diesels in 1957 when a batch of Class 08s were constructed there. For enthusiasts of my era, the Works are intimately linked with the Class 55 "Deltics" which were overhauled there throughout their lives. In terms of new builds, the Class 56 and Class 58 stand out as Doncaster's last major construction projects. The 56s numbered 56031 to 56115 were built at Doncaster between May 1977 and December 1983, whilst the 50-strong Class 58s were completed between 1982 and 1987. Repair and rebuild work at Doncaster slumped quite dramatically after this and much of the site was demolished in 2008 and covered in new housing. Part of the former site is still used by the Wabtec Corporation for carriage and wagon work.

Class	Locos
03	2173, 03061, 03079, 03091, 03151 & 03152
08	3001, 3024, 3028, 3053, 08052, 08056, 08076, 08092, 08100, 08260, 08268, 08401, 08404, 08420, 08444, 08495, 08514, 08554, 08555, 08706 & 08782
12	12127
13	13001
31	31102, 31145, 31154, 31172, 31216, 31217, 31226, 31244, 31251, 31252, 31259, 31306, 31307, 31321 & 31322
37	37009, 37039, 37053, 37092, 37106, 37183, 37186, 37235, 37256 & 37267
55	55011, 55013, 55015 & 55018
84	84001 & 84008

Table 23: Locos present at Doncaster Works on 27 July 1974.

Above: On 7 January 1977, shortly after having arrived brand new from Romania, 56006 stands outside Doncaster Works. Between January and May 1977 the first 11 of the Romanian-built Class 56s had to visit the works for remedial work.

Right: On 26 October 1991, Murray Brown, the Editor of Rail, stands proudly next to Judy, the magazine's secretary, as they unveil the nameplate on 31116, named in honour of the magazine's first ten years.

Left, below & bottom: These three views of the Works, on the day of the "Rail" naming, show the variety of work being undertaken at Doncaster, as well as some of the stock that was scrapped there. In the main workshop 47704 stands alongside 56038 which is undergoing a major overhaul, with Thornaby's 47363 to the right. The second view shows a mixture of freight locomotives and DMUs which from left to right are 56067, 144014, 58047 and a Western Region Pressed Steel DMU carriage. Finally outside is 20157 and a single car DMU awaiting scrapping.

WATH

It was always a bit of a challenge to get to Wath as it was a 60-minute walk from Mexborough, although there was a bus service to shorten the journey. The depot there was built in 1951, as part of the electrification of the Woodhead Route from Manchester. By 1963, when the electric locomotives used on the route were all allocated to Reddish in South Manchester, the depot continued to maintain diesels and accommodate the electric Class 76s used on freight over the Pennines. The Woodhead Line closed in July 1981 and the depot at Wath survived until 1983, when it was closed. The shed building then became an industrial unit, but was eventually demolished in the early 1990s. There was one major stabling point linked to Wath; Rotherwood Sidings which was the other eastern extremity of the electrified route. This too was difficult to get to as it was a 45-minute walk from Woodhouse station. I only visited it once and to my shame I didn't record all the locomotive numbers,

although I did take one or two photographs. A sample finding at the depot in the mid-1970s is given in Table 24.

Class	Locos
08	08048, 08049, 08050, 08051, 08504, 08729, 08864, 08865 & 08866
25	25016 & 25017
31	31298
37	37105, 37127, 37137, 37139, 37170, 37171 & 37226
76	76037

Table 24: Locos present at Wath on 9 August 1975.

Below: On 15 April 1980, fresh out of Doncaster Works, 56075 stands beside 76035, 76038, 76006, 76021 and 76022 at Wath depot.

Below: By 26 May 1985, the disused Wath shed building was still standing and being used as an industrial unit, as seen on the right of this view. 20167 and 20174 stand in the sad remnants of the once massive double hump yard with 6T36, the afternoon trip freight to Tinsley. Alongside them is 08872 with the 6T60 trip from Wath to Manvers Coking Plant.

Above: On 16 August 1982, in the time when only diesels were serviced at Wath, the line up there was 31141 and 31116, with 20095, 20066 and 31311 to their right.

Above: Seven examples of the Class 76 electrics were to be found on Rotherwood stabling point on 23 September 1980. For reasons I cannot fathom 41 years later, I did not record their numbers.

TINSLEY

Tinsley was one of the top half dozen diesel depots in the UK which had allocations of 200 or more engines and could guarantee the visitor over 70 locomotives on shed every weekend. It was also a depot I frequently visited because one could make a trip from Cardiff and combine it with a visit to Toton on a Saturday and perhaps one more Midlands depot, yielding at least 250 numbers in a day! I would take 1E32, the 07.45 Cardiff–Newcastle to Sheffield, before finding the bus stop for the 40-minute journey on a No. 24 to Brinsworth, Three Magpies. From here one hurried up the hill and over the bridge spanning the west end of the reception

sidings at Tinsley Yard. The depot had a conveniently located footpath along its southern perimeter which allowed locomotives to be recorded. I also found over the years that it was relatively easy to pop in and make sure one collected all the numbers of the locomotives inside the classic six-road main shed, which could hold up to 24 main line engines.

The depot at Tinsley opened in 1964 as part of the much larger project to concentrate freight marshalling at the new automated Tinsley Hump Yard and goods traffic at the new Sheffield International Freight Terminal. For the first two decades of

its life it remained busy servicing freight locomotives and also some of the Class 45s that worked the Sheffield to St. Pancras express services. In 1984 however, the start of an inexorable decline began, with the closure of the hump at Tinsley Yard. Traffic had been falling for some years but the 1984 Miners' Strike was the death knell for hump shunting at Tinsley. The engine shed continued to service locomotives, most notably for Railfreight Distribution, for whom it produced several celebrity liveries and finely turned out named locomotives. The collapse of Speedlink in 1990 and the subsequent privatisation of BR led to the depot's doors being closed in 1998. It has since been demolished and a car showroom occupies some of the land. There were four stabling points linked to Tinsley at Darnall, Sheffield Station, Rotherham Station and Beighton Permanent Way Yard. Table 25 gives a couple of sample observations from 1974.

Class	Locos on 16 April 1974	Locos on 1 June 1974
08	08008, 08033, 08186, 08208, 08219, 08244, 08386, 08538 & 08575	08008, 08024, 08033, 08075, 08076, 08115, 08185, 08186, 08260, 08266, 08460, 08507, 08749, 08860, 08862, 08866, 08877 & 08880
13	13001, 13002 & 13003	13001, 13002 & 13003
20	8314, 20056, 20059, 20129, 20130, 20131, 20206, 20213 & 20215	20003, 20023, 20057, 20091, 20121, 20129, 20206, 20207, 20209, 20211 & 20213
25	25012, 25018, 25019, 25022, 25034, 25083, 25089, 25107, 25198 & 25213	25016, 25024, 25025, 25033, 25034, 25083, 25089, 25090, 25091, 25098, 25206 & 25210
31	31227	31172, 31274 & 31301
37	37103, 37104, 37108, 37116 & 37123	37071, 37081, 37089, 37101, 37106, 37117, 37124, 37127, 37136, 37172 & 37209
40	40084	40038
45	45104	69
47	1838, 47022, 47038, 47044, 47047, 47103, 47212, 47292, 47297, 47314 & 47433	47049, 47166, 47169, 47174, 47276, 47281 & 47297

Table 25: Locos present at Tinsley on two dates in 1974.

Left: During late 1989 and 1990, the disused secondary sorting sidings at Tinsley Yard were used to store withdrawn locomotives. On 2 January 1990, this panorama reveals 35 locomotives. The left-hand row contains from front to back 47412, 45130, 20226, 20126 and 47017. The next row along contains 45140, 45145, 47093, 45115 and 47104. The third row across has 45033, 45150, 45120, 968024, 45134, 45124, 46009 and 45052. The fourth row comprises of 45046, 97413, 97410, 97412, 45113, 97409, 45107, 45110 and 97411. The final row houses 45007, 45037, 45012, 45106, 45128, 45141, 45103 and 47130.

Below: During the week commencing Monday 22 July 1974, I stayed with a family friend in Sheffield. The following four images are some of the reproducible images taken during the evenings of that week. Each day I went out round Yorkshire, visiting as many depots as possible and upon my return at tea time I headed to Tinsley to record the locomotives there. 25085, 25018, 25084, 25083 and 25090 stand in a row at the east end of Tinsley Depot on 22 July 1974, with 31298 visible at the end of the line.

Above: One of my favourite pre-SLR images is this shot taken on a sunny 24 July 1974. 20204, 20023, 20215, 20003, 20133, 20201, 20203, 20058 and 20091 stretch out eastwards at Tinsley. To their left, Class 45 No. 136 and 08075 are two more of the 55 locos on shed that evening.

Above: 37107 sits alongside 24085 and 24054 on 25 July 1974, when 54 locomotives could be found on shed at Tinsley.

Left: Looking along the same line up in the other direction on 22 July 1974, 31298 stands at the head of the row of Class 25s listed above. To their right are 47169, 37088, 47121, 08878 and Class 45 No. 102. That evening there were 47 locomotives on the depot.

Above: On 12 January 1978, a friend from school and I were invited for medical school interviews in Sheffield (we both ended up studying medicine in Cambridge). Our interviews went quickly and so I suggested we took advantage of the sun and snow and take the bus to The Three Magpies at Brinsworth! The five photographs on these two pages are a selection of those recorded that day as we wandered around Tinsley. Firstly, 13002 stands outside the west end of the main shed at Tinsley. This locomotive was comprised of two former Class 08s.

Above right: The original Romanian Class 56, 56001, was undergoing load tests as I recall and was parked at the depot with a test carriage.

‖ **Below:** 20022 stands with all its side hatches open, between 37122 on its left and 45061 to its right.

‖ **Below:** To the right of 20022 and 45061 in the next bay are 20129 and 20061.

‖ **Left:** Looking towards the main shed from the east end of the complex, this line up contains, from left to right, 45030, 08183, 08260, 08386, 08223, 08331, 37052 and finally 37108.

Above: The four images on this two-page spread were taken on a dreary 4 July 1990 and have been included because I was able to take some reasonable views inside the maintenance shed. 60013 was amongst the first of the class to arrive at Tinsley and was there for crew familiarisation. Behind it is 45106 which had been withdrawn and had smashed windows. It had previously been stored in Tinsley Yard as the January 1990 image on pages 86 & 87 shows and it is not known why it had been brought up to the main shed. In any case, it was cut up at Booths of Rotherham in 1992.

Above: Inside, the depot was full, with all the roads occupied predominantly by Railfreight Distribution (RfD) locomotives. 47377 is seen alongside 31160 and 37504.

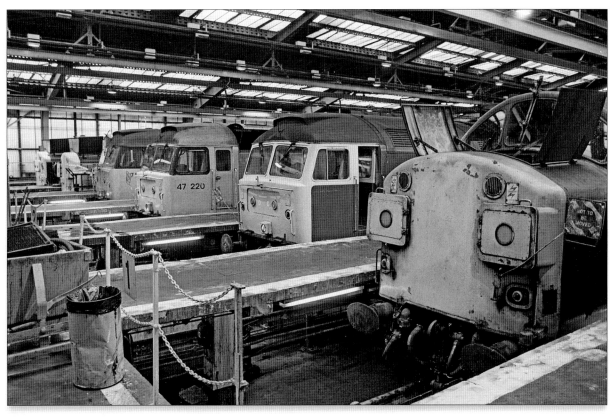

Above: Sadly I did not record the numbers of the engines seen at the front end of the packed maintenance shed, so can only say that 47220 was present. The line up is very representative of the time, with RfD Class 47s and Class 37s filling the shed.

Above: 37032 carried the unofficial name "MIRAGE" which had been painted on by Tinsley's staff. The celebrity loco sits in the only bay with space at the west end of the shed, while to the left is 47016, which carried the name "The Toleman Group".

Below, right & below right: A couple of weeks later, on 18 July 1990, and the sun is out. This panorama at the eastern end of the complex shows 08749, 08919, 09008 and 09013 in the foreground, with 47293, 47120, 47009, 47012, 47338 and 47445 behind and to their left. The row of 47s to the right of the shunters includes 47012, 47451 and 47100 and at least three more 47s can be made out inside the depot building. In the second image, 09013 displays another of the unofficial names that were applied by Tinsley's staff. It was one of the 09s that were transferred away from BR's Southern Region when the freight work there collapsed. The higher maximum speed of the 09s made them ideal for short-distance local trip freights, such as on the Uskmouth branch in Newport and to Shepcote Lane Steelworks in Sheffield, hence the unofficial naming of 09013. The third image from that day shows that the western end of the main shed was relatively deserted, with just 37110 and 08880 stabled outside.

Above: The refuelling and inspection shed alongside the sorting sidings at Tinsley was still busy on 18 July 1990. 47485 had just arrived with a freight and heads for the refuelling point. Amongst the locomotives stabled alongside the shed are 20178, 31280 and 45106. Having seen the state of the Class 45 just two weeks earlier, as illustrated above, I suspect that all four locomotives stabled there were in fact withdrawn from service.

Below: It was almost exclusively shunting locomotives that would be stabled in the sidings to the south of Sheffield Midland station. On 5 August 1978, 08287, 08879 and 08543 were found there.